The Pizza Shop

Written by Sarah Smith
Photography by Michael Curtain

 sundance

I love pizza.

My friend Kelly loves
pizza, too.

Kelly's uncle, Charlie, owns a pizza shop.
Last week we spent a whole day at his shop.

We arrived at the pizza shop early.
It was quiet and dark inside.

Charlie turned on the lights and the pizza oven.

There were lots of things that he had to do before the shop opened at lunchtime. We wanted to help.

First Charlie made the fresh pizza dough. The dough is made from flour, yeast, sugar, water, and salt.

Then he mixed the dough in the blender and let it sit for 30 minutes, until it grew bigger.

When the dough was ready, Charlie pulled off pieces. He weighed them to make sure that they were all the same size. Each piece was rolled into a ball that was ready to be used to make the pizza crust.

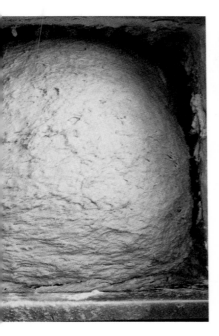

Every week there is a
delivery of large bags
of flour, boxes of cheese,
ham, salami, and big
cans of tomatoes and
olives.

Charlie uses the tomatoes to make a sauce
to put on the pizza crusts. He makes
enough tomato sauce to last for a few days
and keeps it in the refrigerator.

9

Kelly and I went to the market with Charlie to buy peppers, onions, mushrooms, and herbs.

We helped to choose the freshest peppers.

When we got back to the shop, Charlie prepared the ingredients for the pizzas.

olives   sliced mushrooms

dried tomatoes   peppers   grated cheese

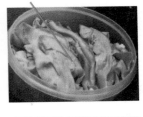

capers   ham

anchovies   pineapple

artichokes

While Charlie worked in the kitchen,
Kelly and I helped to get the shop ready.

14

Charlie gave us a stack of flat cardboard sheets to fold into boxes. The boxes will be used for take-out pizzas.

Each day Charlie chooses a "Special of the Day." Sometimes he asks Kelly to choose the pizza of the day, but today he asked me. I chose ham, cheese, tomatoes, and olives.

At lunchtime, Kelly's aunt, Nancy, arrived
to help Charlie. Now the shop was ready
to open.

Nancy took the orders, while Charlie made the pizzas. He took a ball of pizza dough and threw it in the air to stretch it. He put tomato sauce on the pizza crust and sprinkled cheese on top. Then he added the toppings the customer asked for. Charlie then put each pizza into the oven.

The pizza oven cooked the top and the
bottom of the pizza at the same time.

Nancy took each pizza out of the oven when it was ready. Then she cut it into slices for the customer.

Later that afternoon, when it was quiet again, Charlie let us make our own pizzas. Kelly and I each took a ball of dough. I threw mine in the air like Charlie showed us, but it didn't work. So Charlie fixed the dough for both of us.

I put tomato sauce, lots of cheese, ham, and olives on my pizza. Kelly put fruit on hers.

At six o'clock, my mother came to pick me up. "Guess what?" she said. "We're having pizza for dinner tonight!"